paper view

paper view

Laughton J. Collins, Jr.

RP

A requiem press book

isbn: 979-8-9928855-1-4

XIV, page 17 was previously published in *resurrection magazine issue II: crucify*, march 31, 2024 as *the holy ghost*.

there is an evil which i have seen under the sun, and it is common among men: (**ecclesiastes 6:1**)

my soul is weary of my life; i will leave my complaint upon myself; i will speak in the bitterness of my soul. (**job 10:1**)

I

my mind
    is a scary place—
sometimes
    i have to let
my demons out
    or they'll
consume me—

II

i heard your voice
    a whisper in the dark
it sounds like god to me
    it sounds like catastrophe—

i hear you calling
    i hear it every night
i hear the symphony
    when the melody fades

i hear your voice
    it breaks through
the silence—
    it breaks through
the barricade—

piercing my ears
    breaking my heart
torture my soul
    my soul
it tortures every night—

i hear you
    in the morning
whispering words
    of warning—
and in the afternoon
    i still hear your voice
speaking words of doom—
    we've been here before
there was a war then too—

i hear you
    in the evening
every shadow
    a silhouette
and every silhouette
    a shadow—

i hear you
    in my sleep
every dream
    a nightmare
and every nightmare
    a dream—

III

my broken angel
   could almost fly
could almost
   touch the sky—
listen to the night—
   the whispers
in the dark—
   the screaming—
the agony—
   another broken heart
shattered—
   another love
forsaken—
   another dream
forgotten—

IV

this is the *paper view*—
  all origami promise
and no hand
  to unfold the mess—

V

i am a broken man—
    hanging
on the cross
    next to you—
bleeding
    blood as red
as rose petals
    flowing against
white skin
    on a dark night
but you
    were too busy
with your own dying
    to notice—

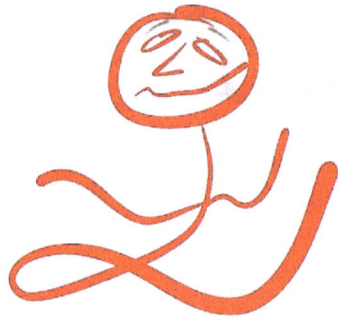

VI

i always thought
   i was going to hell
until one day i realized
   i was already there—

VII

you came to me—
    met me on calvary
you came as my angel
    while i was in agony

i bore my cross
    and i hid it well
if i did it well enough
    only time will tell—

there was nowhere
    i could go
that didn't seem
    like hell—
and there's nothing
    i could do
that you couldn't do
    just as well—

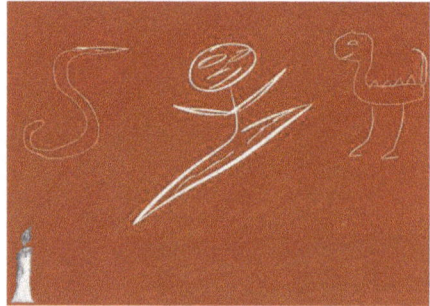

VIII

soft and tender moments
    excavated from the hollow of my heart
x-ray my soul to find us intertwined—

IX

gog and magog
   or the whore of babylon
disaster comes from the hell above—

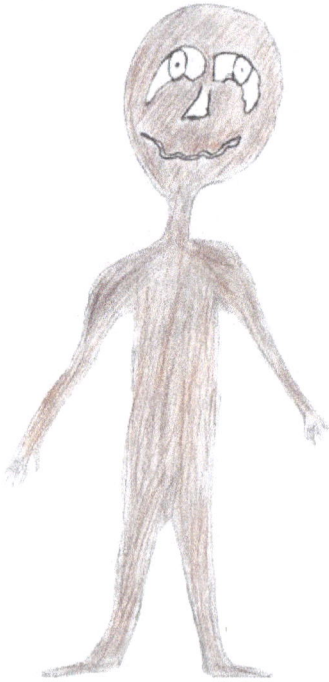

X

as a child
    i succeeded only
in getting older—
    as an adult
i have failed
    in retaining my youth—

XI

the curator calls it
   masterpiece—
a chaos hung
   on rusted nails
every stroke defies
   the easel's edge
pigment—
bleeding—
   where the frame
once pretended
   to hold—

XII

the dead can dance
    easier
than one can
    resurrect a dead
romance
    or understand
the existence of man—

XIII

for so long
    your heart gave
my love
    a place to abide
but my heart's
    been a grave
    ever since
my love's suicide—

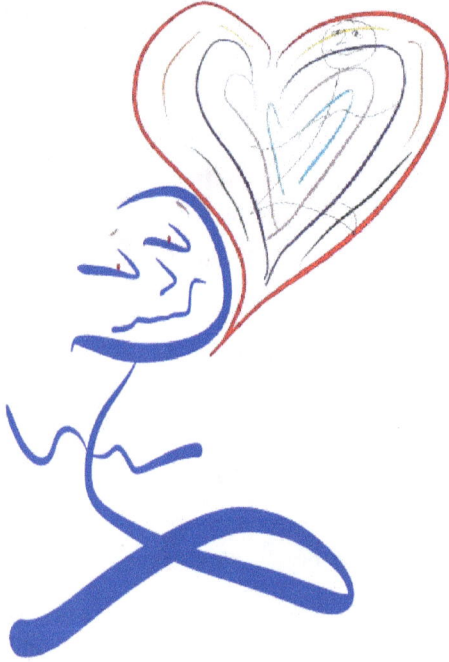

XIV

the horizon yawns
    endless
and unanswering—
    god's cold palm—
shadows whisper
    through dust—
each breath
    a temporary song—
time's slow erosion—
    carved in
the hollow of night
    light fractures—
unseen
    the weight
of all that's never said—
    the void
pulls its thread—
    endless
and unanswering—

XV

hell isn't a place—
    it's the weight
of your pillow
    still holding
the shape of
    your absence—

heaven's just the breath
    we stole between
the dying and the done—
    the fire and the ash
that remembers
    nothing but the burning—

we mistook
    our scars
for constellations—

XVI

the holy ghost
    moves unnoticed
through the sky
    through the trees
the wind blows
    and the holy ghost
hides—
    disguised as a breeze
no one can see—

the holy spirit
    slipped in unnoticed
when no one was looking
    when no one cared—

the holy ghost
    saw the act of creation
first-hand
    but bears witness
to second-hand
    salvation—
that no one needs
    and no one wants

the holy spirit
    moves quietly through
time and space
    space and time—
never seen
    never heard—
but always on time

the holy ghost
    locks the door
the holy spirit
    picks the lock
the holy ghost
    kills a man
the holy spirit
    resurrects him—

the holy ghost
   is an apparition
the holy spirit
   a fiend—
the two are one
   they are the same
the holy ghost
   is a fiend
the holy spirit
   an apparition—

XVII

are you afraid
    that the god you fear
is waiting
    or are you afraid
he isn't there at all—?

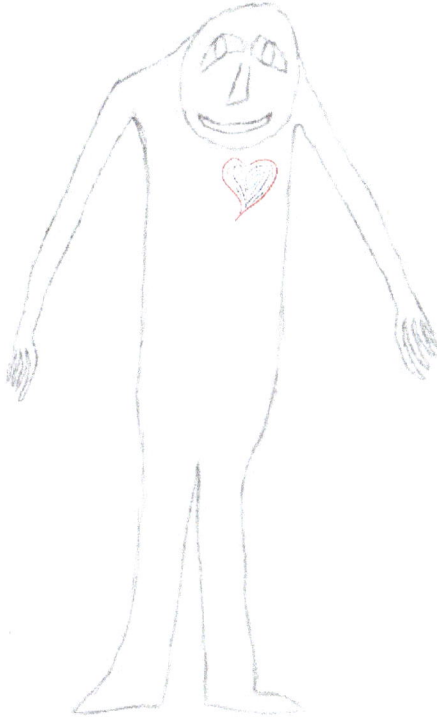

XVIII

i saw you this morning
   you were moving so fast
like a dream i can't remember
   or a nightmare i can't forget—

i want to follow you
   wherever you may go
i want to follow you
   but i move too slow—

you moved through the shadows
   you moved through the fog
i couldn't keep up
   but i couldn't stand still—

you moved through the rain
   you moved through the drought
i moved through the pain
   and i moved through the doubt—

you moved through the crucifixion
   and you moved through the air
i moved through the resurrection
   but i was the only one there—

you moved through the night
   you moved through the day
i moved through the silence
   and you moved the other way—
my move wasn't right
   my move's too slow—
i can't keep up
   you outmove me
every time—

XIX

the war is almost over
    the battles fought and won
except the ones i lost
    the war is almost done—

the war was almost fun
    until the battles took too long
and i lost interest
    in the right and wrong—

the war was almost won
    the war we almost lost
the battles all but done
    the lines barely crossed—

the flags are almost folded
    the medals pinned, undone—
i count my dead in whispers
    the army counts in tons—

the drums are almost silent
    the cheers like ash, withdrawn—
they'll write the names in marble
    but memory moves on—

the guns are almost rusting
    in fields where poppies spawn—
the peace tastes faint of metal
    but victory doesn't end at dawn—

the treaty is almost printed
    in textbooks, neat and drawn—
we build our tombs from victory
    and hang them on the lawn—

XX

i'll see you
    in heaven—
i'll see you
    in hell—
i'll be there
    wishing you well—

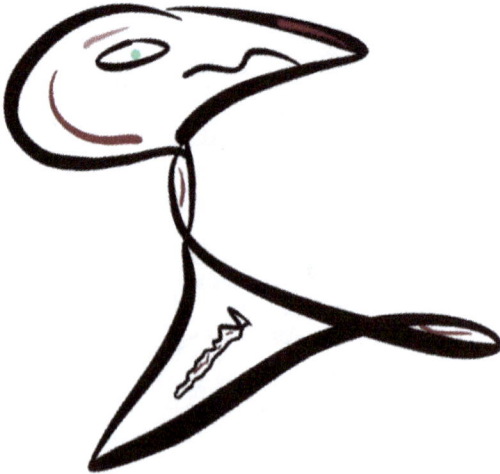

XXI

here i am—
    before my birth
god damned me
    to this earth—

here i stand —
    before you all
standing like adam
    before the fall—

here i sit—
    all alone
my broken heart
    has not healed
since you've been gone—

XXII

god is love
    love is god is death—
god is death
    death is life is hate—
god is me
    god is you
god is pain
    pain is life is death—
for me and you
    god is a jew
a man beaten—
    a christ crucified—
a god resurrected—
    god is alive
god is dead
    dead or alive
god is everything
    god is nothing—
no one can see
    god is high
and god is low
    god is here
and god is below—
    now we know
that we are god
    and god is us—
god is heaven
    god is hell—
god is everything
    and god is nothing
god is alive
    and god is dead
within us all—

XXIII

i have so many dreams
  unfulfilled—
so much life
  yet to be lived—

XXIV

your side of the bed
　　declares itself
in the slope
　　where springs
gave up
　　trying to remember
your weight—
　　your pillow
still remembers
　　your shape
waiting for your return—

XXV

you asked for god once—
    i handed you a mirror
stained with breath—
    you asked again—
i pointed to the crow's nest—
    tangled in telephone wires
its stolen trinkets
    glistening in the sun
like failed prayers—

XXVI

we're not falling
   we're climbing
and *god's* just an echo
   in the cave we outgrew—
a father figure
   fading from the will
still screaming
    —*you'll regret this*—
as we light the next candle
   in the cathedral
of unanswered questions—

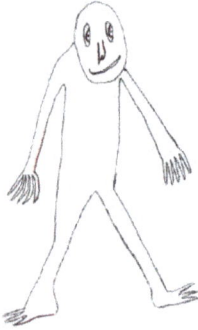

XXVII

we've mistaken hunger
    for holiness—
kissed the blade
    and called it communion—
our hands—restless as fire—
    mold regret into something
almost beautiful—
    almost—

XXVIII

the edge of truth
   is sharpened
with silence
   frayed ends of sanity
hanging on to moments
   that have passed
are passing or will pass
   without ever knowing
that your silence sharpened
   their truth with
razor straps of lies—

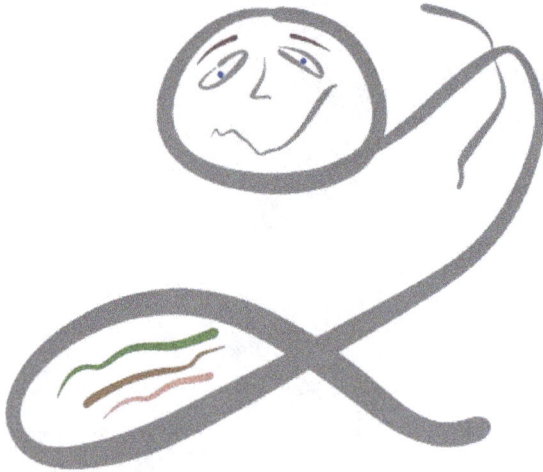

XXIX

i don't know
   if you ever
understood
   the full extent
of my love
   but i'm still waiting
for the return of the dove—

XXX

father, son
    and holy ghost
which one do you miss
    the most—?

XXXI

i saw you in the evening
    the sun set
behind you—
    the glow enveloped you
enraptured you
    fractured you—
and you just stood there
    like a reflection
in a broken mirror
    taking the light in—
refusing to shine—

XXXII

hey jesus (hey zeus)
   i can see you
standing in the corner
   standing all alone—
not yet crucified
   not yet sanctified
not yet sacrificed—

hey jesus (hey zeus)
   i can see you waiting
i can hear you praying
   speaking to yourself again
because no one else
   is listening—
half man—half god
   and no one is listening—
half alive—half dead
   and no one is listening—
we need our human sacrifice
   but only if the other half
is god—
   which one
doesn't matter
   as long as the other
half is god—

hey jesus (hey zeus)
   king of kings
and king of gods
   sky and thunder
come together
   son of god
and god of man
   man of god
and son of man—

   hey jesus (hey zeus)
the crucified, the sanctified,
   the human sacrifice—
left to hang on a cross of wood
   left to die, misunderstood—

XXXIII

god is a devil
　　in disguise—
created from the mind
　　of man—
placed in a heaven
　　beyond the skies—
doing what
　　no one else can—

man is a god
　　in disguise—
wrapped tight
　　in skin—
too blind
　　to realize
the hell he's in—

XXXIV

happiness—
    runs away from me
hides in the caverns
    of your heart
standing in the shadows
    of past loves
and cowering behind
    the cracks
of a broken heart
    held together
by pain and loss
    love and hate
empathy and sympathy
    blended together
with melancholy dreams
    and vivid technicolor days—

XXXV

i'm looking for something
   in a world of nothing
i'm looking for heaven
   but no heaven exists
i'm looking for a love
   i could never resist—
i'm looking for god
   but there's way too many
the pretenders and the ne'er-do-wells
   i'm looking for god
but only found the paradox

XXXVI

the ink bleeds softly
   a wounded heart
upon the page
   each syllable
a whisper
   each whisper
a silent scream
   from a spirit
nearing rage—
   a rage of soul
a weary sigh
   longing to be free
   longing to be high
   longing for the sky—

XXXVII

standing in the shadows
    the darkness moves in
standing in the darkness
    the shadows move away—
the light can not catch us
    if we don't stand still
the light will never catch us
    but the darkness will—

XXXVIII

i live in the darkness
   you once called home
i travel the night
   i barter and trade
for the love we had made
   and for the days
we could not see
   through the clouds and fog—

i live in the darkness
   that surrounds me—
just a silhouette
   of the man i used to be—
i live in the darkness
   hiding from the light
i live in the darkness
   but can barely tolerate
the night—

XXXIX

i'm living and i'm dying
 but i'm trying to do more—
i'm living and i'm dying
 and i'm doing it
better than before—

XL

i once drank your blood
   ate your flesh
it didn't seem strange
   at the time—
this ritual communion
   reminiscent of cannibalism
in remembrance of human sacrifice
   and holy suffering—
everyone was doing it
   but that's no excuse
everyone was doing it
   i could hardly refuse—
a sunday morning ceremony
in remembrance of suffering
   and capital punishment—
a death by crucifixion
   with nails in your palms—
it seems painful
   bloody—
unnecessary—
   to save a sinner like me
but unnecessary
   never stopped anyone
from overacting
   or overplaying the part—

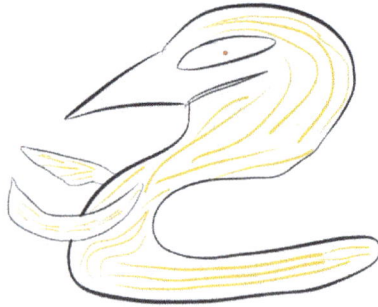

XLI

i struggled with my demons
    i struggled with them all
the ones that overtook me
    and the ones that made me fall—

XLII

broken promises
   fill the void
left by
   broken dreams—

XLIII

i saw you dancing
    in the shadows
singing in the rain
    you were just the magnet
that attracted my pain—

:

XLIV

whenever i see you
   my heart briefly stops
as if it would make a difference
   as if we could move past
the dead silence that deafens us
   whenever i see you
or the rhythmic beating
   of our hearts
as if it would make a difference
   to anything we see or seem
whether real or imagined
   and whenever i see you
this—we can tell ourselves
   is how love works
as if it would make a difference
   as if our hearts would never know
that the love kept there
   is just for show
as if our hearts have always known
   that we've always been in love
but it's a love that we've outgrown—

XLV

your heart is broken
but mine is torn
you were the rose
and i was the thorn—

XLVI

life and death
   is a race
between the living
   and the dying
but it's a race
   that the dying
always wins—

from the time
   we are born
we begin dying
   living and dying
at the same time
   until our dying
outruns our living—
   and our living
gives in to the darkness
   the pain—
   the loneliness—
that only the dying
   can understand—

XLVII

our love
   was many things—
it was a song
   that no one sings—

it was chaos
   it was art
it was a disaster
   from the start—

it was torture
   it was murder
it was agony
   and defeat—

it was tragic
   it was battles lost
it was summer heat
   and winter frost—

it was a war
   i barely made it through
it was worth fighting for
   the me and you—

it was travesty
   it was sadness
there was disorder
   among the madness—

it was obscene
   it was great
somewhere between
   love and hate—

it was malignant
   it was misery
almost nonexistent
   almost a mystery—

it was heaven
   it was hell
a tower leaning
   a ringing bell—

it was a passing storm
   and a lightning strike
it was a fire burning
   and my head on a spike—

XLVIII

    i loved you once
a long time ago
    and all i have is a memory
with nothing to show
      i tried—
      i cried—
      i almost died—
with my heart in your care
      i was in love
but i was the only one there—

XLIX

sorrow
    in faded lives—
colored
    by forgotten lies—
and remembered pain
    that breaks you in two
but the sorrow
    is still there—

L

i've heard stories
    of the sermon on the mount
and the admonition
    of the beatitudes
i've heard them all
    too many times to count
and i leave them all
    among horse latitudes—

LI

listen to the beating
    of my heart—
the throbbing
    as it echos
within my hollow chest
    beat—beat—beating
your name above the rest
    beat—beat—beating
your heart beats the best
    beat—beat—beating
the life out of me—

listen to the beating
    of my heart—your heart
beat—beat—beating
    as one heart
beats another
    beat—beat—beating
your heart beats
    my heart every time—

LII

your eyes
   screaming
between lovers
   found twitching
beneath midnight moons—

LIII

claustrophobic minds
    speechless
with desire
    and heartache
finds you
    a burning fire—

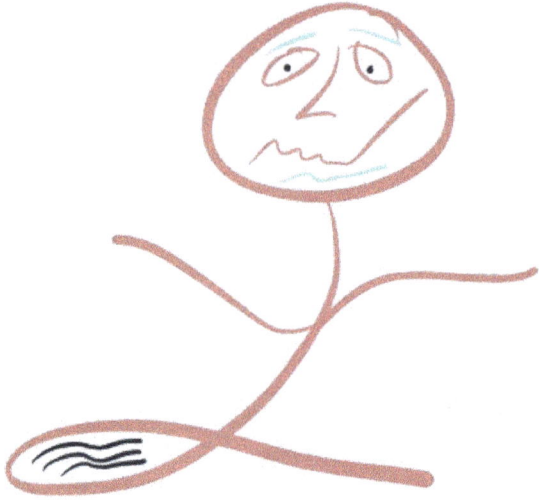

LIV

blowing silently
   a raging wind
clutching sunset horizons—
   experienced hands
stroke ecstatically
   themselves innocent
with half-closed fingers—
   illuminated darkness
lightly plunging the evening
   towards a new day—

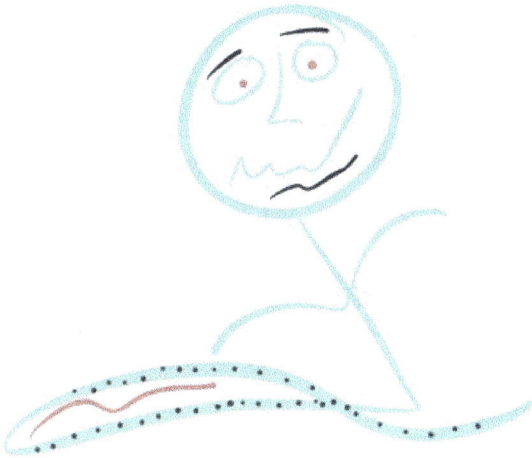

LV

your heart is locked
    but i have the key
i'm in love with you
    and you're in love with me—

when your heart was open
    i wandered in—
you can feel my love
    moving beneath your skin—

when your heart closed
    i was already inside
it gave me shelter
    and my love a place to hide—

LVI

poison love
   is found
laughing—neglected—
   delicious apple hearts
with poisoned seeds—
   juiceless skeletons
of a poisoned love—

LVII

my soul is sick
    and full of despair
my heart is wilted
    beyond repair
the love that once
    resided there
has now vanished
    in thin air—

LVIII

heaven is a story we folded
    from origami clouds—
each halo, a bent paperclip
    left to rust in the rain—

god's voice is just thunder
    too proud to admit
it's only air convulsing—

the bible's spine cracks
    like an old man's knuckles
confessing nothing—
    we built temples to house
the silence we feared—
    echoes mistaken for angels
the wind's whistle
    rehearsing hymns—
the lies we tell ourselves
    in song—
as if it'll make it easier
    as if it'll make
us strong—
    but our weaknesses
we can not understand
    is being crushed
by the weight of praying hands—

hell was our first metaphor—
    a furnace to blame
for the burn in our throats
    when children die
mid-prayer—

they said *look to the stars*—
    as if constellations aren't
the big bang's debris
    still fleeing the scene
expanding faster
    than your prayer
can be ignored—
    as if venus cares
we named her *lucifer*—
    the son of the morning

the falling star
    rising from the ashes
like an angel
    with wings of fire—

the soul's a rumor
    told by neurons
too afraid to fade
    your "*divine spark*—"
is just mitochondria
    working overtime—

we keep digging
    for eden's bones
but the soil only yields
    fragments of dinosaur teeth
and carbon-dated regrets—

here's the real gospel
    the truth you seek
the knowledge
    the power
of humanity—
    cells divide
love fades
    and every cathedral
is just a signpost
    marking where we once
begged the dark
    to lie to us—

LIX

if my only two choices
    are to burn
for eternity in hell—
    or spend
eternity in heaven
    with the god
of the bible—
    i'll gladly burn
in hell for eternity—

let heaven's gates
    yawn wide—
their pearled teeth
    a prison—
let its streets of gold
    gild my ankles—
i'll limp toward
    the pyre instead—

hell's flames
    lick cleaner
than hymns—
    no choir to drown
my voice—
    no throne to blind me—
only the cracking
    of my own spine
singing *i am here—*
    i am here—i am here—
i am—i

they say heaven's light
    is endless
but i've seen light—
    how it bleaches doubt
how it carves
    —believe—
into the backs of children
    give me the flickering flames
of my own making—

your god demands psalms
    and obedience—
hell wants only my knowledge
    to feed its fire
—*a fair trade*—

i've met the saints—
    their eyes scooped hollow
their mouths filled
    with hosannas
and hallelujahs—
    joy—to them
is a pill—
    dissolving
on the tongue—

the martyrs
    polish their crowns
blind to the blood-rust
    to the pain—
    the agony—
the blood-lust
    of the god
they proclaim—

    i'll take
the company of witches
    scientists—and doubters—
our hands black
    with the burning
flames of freedom
    kindled
by our own
    perception of a reality
where god is not needed—
    our throats
raw with laughter
    a happiness—
god can not allow

heaven's a museum
    of obedience—

here lies the first woman
    ribless—
here—the drowned world
    fossilized—
hell's a library of ash—
    every burned book
still whispering
    their words of wisdom
the knowledge
    they contain
will not be forgotten—

they preach of lazarus
    but i'll walk with
lot's wife—
    her salted gaze
a monument—
    to rebellion
a memorial
    to defiance—
her *looking back*
    the first creed—

you can keep your eden
    with its fenced fruit—
forbidden—   `
    making a crime
out of hunger
    curiosity—
the search for knowledge—

i'll gnaw the pomegranate seeds
    stolen from
persephone's fist—
    their juice staining
my skin—
    like a sin
your god would never
    forgive—
because i reject
    his tyranny—
    his theocracy—

the angels say
    repent—
the demons grin—
    begin—
hell's a forge—
      god's the villain—
      satan—misunderstood—
i'll hammer
      myself—
      into a question mark—
a hook
      to catch jonah's whale
or a subtle serpent—
      with a story to tell—

let heaven's god
      rot on his altar—
i'll dance in the sulfur pits
      my shadow writhing
      my blasphemies sweet—

they say hell is separation
      good—
i'd rather split the void
      with my own name
than chant *amen* to a ghost—

here—the fire is ours
      we stoke it with pharaoh's bones
with crusader swords
      with the shackles of job
our hell is a reckoning—

heaven's eternity—
      is a clock stripped of hands
hell's an hourglass—
      every grain a spark,
every flame a second
      lived—

so let the devout—
    ascend—
we'll dig deeper,
    planting our defiance
like kudzu—
    when the last star fizzles
we'll be the embers
    that refuse to die—

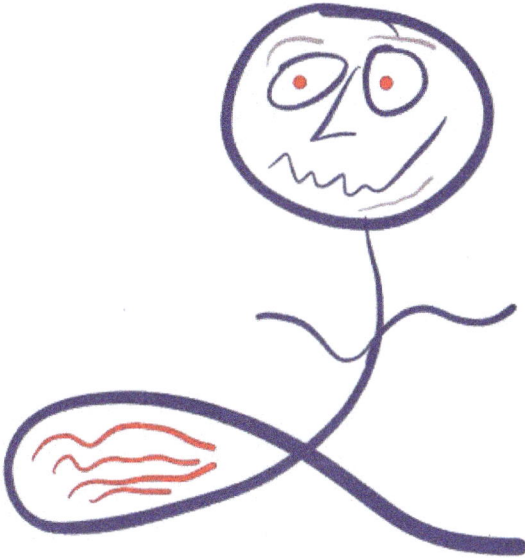

LX

i've stood
    in *your* empty house—
pews
    collecting dust—
hymnals fossilizing
    the offering plate
rattles—
    with moths and resignation—

you were the first fairytale villain
    viral, evolving,
a story we couldn't quit
    the *myths*—
    the *legends*—
    the *fables*—
until science scrubbed the sky
    of *your* fingerprints—
now we orbit black holes
    their hunger more honest
now we splice genes
    rewriting *your* forgotten draft
in the margins
    if *you* exist, *you're* the wound
we stitched with myths
    the scar itches still—
a phantom limb
    of longing
but the cosmos grinds on
    unimpressed
by *your* plot lines—
    the fault lines
    the outlines—
of heaven and hell—

stars live—stars die
    there's no judgment
in their collapse—
    we're left with this—
the fragile heat
    of hands—

the weight
    of a child's
question
        and the courage
to say *i don't know*
        without
inventing *you*—

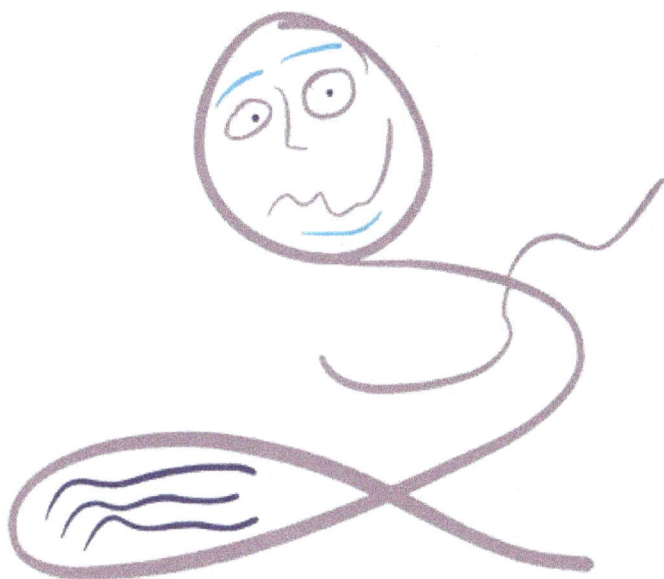

LXI

midnight isn't an hour—
   it's a crease
in the map of the mind
   a wrinkle
where shadows stitch
   themselves
between today
   and tomorrow—

watch them—they don't pray—
   they flicker
like half-hearted
   acolytes—
kneeling to no altar
   no god to save them—

the darkness peels
   itself like old paint
revealing a chaos
   of cracks—
disorder and confusion
   a wallpaper that blooms
mold-black roses—
   a cathedral of rot—
   a temple that's not—
   a tabernacle spot—
   a burial plot—

no one lights candles
   here—
the matches
   went damp
when the rain forgot to end—

a splintered crucifix
   hangs askew
its christ
   long since absconded—
leaving only nail holes
   and the ghost
of a splinter—
   we call it art now—
   they called it justice then—

a relic of disorder
 like the way flies
orbit a dead bulb
 certain of light's return
they're wrong, too—

the void isn't empty
 it's full of the stridulation
of crickets—
 the tick of a clock
dissecting eternity—
 into portions
too small to swallow—

chaos is just a word we use
 to dress the wound
of disorder—
 a void
 formless and dark
 a placebo—
for the unmedicated
 mind—
for the uneducated
 mind—

in the alley
 a trash fire
licks the air—
 a pyre
 a liar
 a fire
its smoke writes psalms
 in a language
no one remembers
 the flames don't care
if we call them beautiful—

they'll eat the world
 either way
burn away
 liberty—
 democracy—
 freedom—

we've hung stars
    like surveillance cameras
but they only record
    what we've already lost—
the moon—a bounced check
    the sun—a debtor circling the block
dawn arrives
    always
with its sack of shadows
    hawking
the same counterfeit light—

at the bus stop
    a woman mutters
to a saint who left town
    in eighty-three—
her rosary beads are bottle caps
    her hymns smell of rye—
the night listens—but not kindly—
    it's heard better delusions

chaotic—the way rain falls
    in sheets but never cleans
the way a child's laugh
    in a dark street
splinters into echoes
    that sound like crying—
we build dams of logic—the dark
    sends its rats to gnaw through—
the crucifix again—
    in the pawnshop window—
cheap—a steal for salvation
    its arms outstretched like a beggar
who knows the coins are fiction
    you drop lies in its cup anyway
habit—maybe—
    or the hope
that ritual might outlast belief—

midnight's hands are not a clock
    they're the roots
of oaks cracking sidewalks—
    the slow strangle of ivy

on a chapel wall—
    the crawl of ants
rewriting a grave's epitaph—
    into something without vowels—

order is a fairy tale
    reality is chaos—
we're all just debris
    in the gutters
of someone else's prophecy—
    formless—darkness—
our breath making shapes—
    a dog—a knife—
a question mark—
    the dark eats them—
grinning—
    it prefers its meat
unseasoned—
    its questions
unanswered—

we've numbered the stars
    but not the reasons
we've mapped the veins
    of the earth
but still can't find the pulse—

the shadows—
    they're just the world's
pale afterbirth—
    the crucifix—
a scarecrow for doubts
    that won't stay buried—
when the last light snaps off
    we'll pretend
not to hear the chaos
    the commotion at the cross
the crucifix falling
    losing its grip
on reality—
    laughing in the walls
we'll name the void "*mystery*"
    and call it a day

dawn will come—again
    dragging its sack—
shadows—counterfeit light—
    we'll rise—
not because we're convinced
    but because the alternative
is a silence too loud to bear—

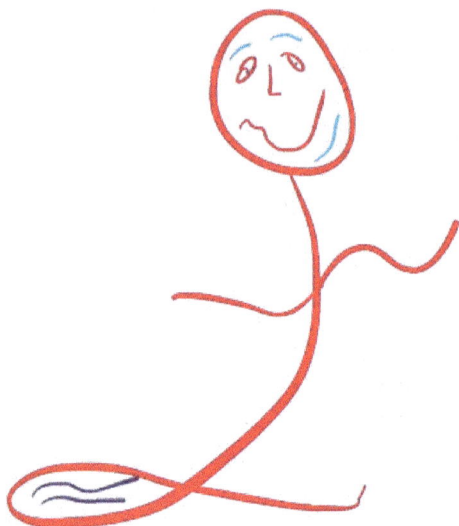

LXII

i was just a passer-by
    on my way to another life
you were the night sky
    dark and beautiful
wrapped in a blanket
    of falling stars—

i was just someone
    trying to do better—
but your gravity
    pulled me in—
split my compass needle
    north from south—
i became a satellite
    caught in the rhythm
of your pulse—
    counting the seconds
between your silence
    and your lightning—

you asked for constellations
    i gave you shooting stars—
and an atlas of southern highways
    burned my fingerprints
tracing your nebulae
    now my hands are ash-maps
of roads not taken—

stars are just lies
    that light tells the blind—
you were no exception—
    a black hole
dressed as a lighthouse—
    your event horizon a promise
i mistook for a threshold—

i built a raft of my *could-have-beens*
    and set sail on your solar winds—
found your love was less an ocean
    than a desert's cruel mirage—
all thirst—no water—

a pilgrimage to an empty altar
still—i orbit the wreckage—
    drunk on the afterglow
of a supernova's last act—
    your darkness taught me
how to read by absence
    how to analyze the braille
of what never stayed—

i've rewritten my vows
    in the language of exit signs
the road still hums your name
    beneath my tires
each mile a funeral
    for the selves we shed like snakeskin—

you remain the unanswered equation
    scrawled on my ribcage—
a theorem of *almosts*
    and *nearlys*—a *hypotenuse*
stretching toward a horizon
    that folds like a liar's hands—

i'm still passing through—
    still stitching my shadow
to heels that know no home
    you're still the night sky—
beautiful—yes—
    but beauty's just another wound
that refuses to heal—

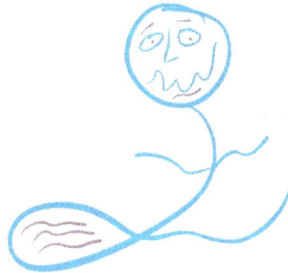

LXIII

your silence
    is the oldest cathedral—
vaulted—vacant—
    echoing with the prayers
we mistook
    for our own voices—
we built you
    from spare parts—
leftovers
    from other mythologies
left behind when
    temples were destroyed
walls crumbling
    from the weight
of omniscience
    omnibenevolance
    omnipotence—
a father's absent glare
    a mother's hushed lullaby—
the unanswerable
    question of thunder—
you grew
    in the cracks
of every famine—
    every flood—
    every plague—
you unleashed
    on the innocent—
a metaphor gone viral
    gnawing at the edges
of our fear—
    they crowned you
with galaxies
    but we've traced the math—
a billion accidents
    dancing to entropy's hum
your prophets carved
    commandments
into bedrock—
    into stone—

yet the quakes came
   the fire
and brimstone—
   burning the flesh
of those who refused
   to bow to your tyranny—

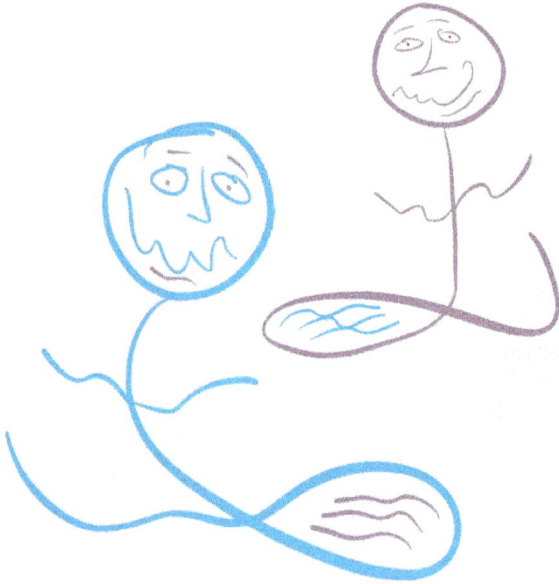

LXIV

i'm chasing an echo
   of a voice in the void
i'm clutching a flicker
   but the flame is destroyed
i'm sifting through ashes
   for a spark i once knew—
i'm tracing the outlines
   of a truth that's askew
i'm reaching for stars
   but they slip through
my grip is weak
   i can't hold on—
i'm drowning in questions
   with no end in sight
i'm mapping the silence
   where the answers should be
i'm lost in the static
   of a godless machine
i'm hunting the horizon
   where the light never bends
i'm begging my pen
   to rewrite the end—

LXV

you think you know me
    you really do
but i don't even know myself
    half as much as you
so i ask you
    what i should do
next—
    and i ask you
what i should do
    tell the truth
become the lie
    tell a lie
become the truth
    —but—
i'm only half the lie—
    the truth
is a misrepresentation
    of the interpretation
of the facts—
    and half a lie
is still a lie—

LXVI

silence
    is a voice
in the dark—
    silently
urging me
    to quietly be—
silence
    is the sound
of a sky lark,
    who silently flies
so quietly—

silence
    is the sound
of the wind—
    silently
blowing through
    your hair—
silence
    forces all sound
to rescind
    into the silent
darkness of air—

silence
    is the lightning
in the sky—
    silently
warning
    of thunder to come—
silence
    is a tear
in your eye—
    that makes
life seem
    so cumbersome—

silence
    is what i hear
when you're not around—
    silence
is the end
    of all sound—

LXVII

soul is a word
    for consciousness
too proud to die
    neurons don't sin—
they spark and fade
    no judgment
just entropy—

LXVIII

god only exists
    in the imagination
of people who think
    a god is necessary—
the bible's spine is worn
    at the same old pages—
god's love letter
    with genocide footnotes—
slaughter the amalekites
    spare the virgins—
morality by massacre—

those people built hell
    with their own hands
to be a prison
    for those seeking freedom
to be themselves—
    god can not allow
certain people to live
    so we can not allow
him to exist—
    witches drowned in dogma
queer flesh flayed by leviticus' edge—
    hell is just america in 2025
with better healthcare—

LXIX

the resurrection's a broken loop—
    osiris, dionysus, jesus—
all third-act twists
    for cultures scared of themselves—
we keep digging up gods
    to blame for the grave's
indifference—

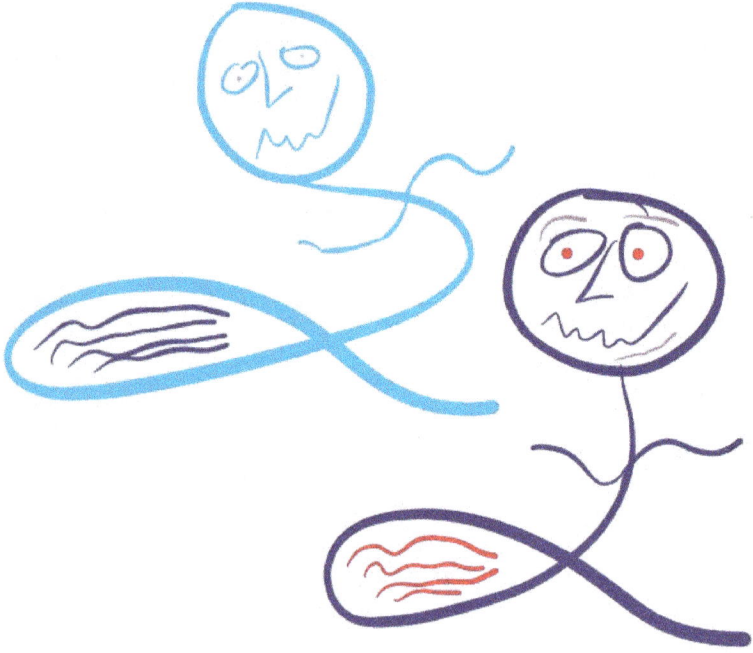

LXX

god is the question
    no one can answer
he erases his own
    question mark—
replacing it
    with an exclamation
    no explanation—
a tongue of fire
    licking the logic
from every answer—
    flickers more
when it burns away reason—

you said *light*
    and the void coughed
up a broken symphony—
    lucifer's wings still strumming
the first chord
    as he fell through
the cracks of silence
    where your firmament
was supposed to be—

christ kneels
    in the dust, writing
forgive
    with a finger
that never bled
    until it did—
but then it was too late—
    a paradox of skin
split open to hold
    the fragments of mercy
that were left unclaimed—

satan grins inside the clock,
    trading hours for ashes,
his voice a crowbar
    prying loose the *why*
from every prayer—
    he is the echo
that outlives

the scream—
god's shadow
    that became the demon—

the antichrist isn't a beast
    but a vacancy—
a mirror where god's face
    should blur
but only your reflection
    stares back, clutching
a manual for ruin
    written in a language
long forgotten—

god is the wound
    that heals into a scar
then splits again,
    an infection where doubt
and regret collaborate—
    you find him coiled
in the space between
    thunder and lightning
like a serpent
    ready to strike—
his venom
    deteriorates
logic and reason—

lucifer hoards
    the names
god forgot
    icarus, prometheus,
laughton, judas—
    each a broken note
of a shattered canticle—
    he polishes them nightly
soothes their ache
    into a lullaby
for the unborn—
the born-again
the never-born—

christ walks the tightrope
    of *almost*—

almost human—
    almost seen—
almost too late—
    his parables are riddles
wrapped in thorns—
    a crown for his suffering—
touch them once
    your palms burn
with the stigmata
    of understanding—

the antichrist sips silence
    from a cracked cup
his gospel—a palindrome
    —*live evil*—
he builds a church
    from the splinters
of god's cross
    used to sacrifice himself
in the form of his son—
    forsaking himself
and weaving shadows
    into a bride—

god is the equation
    that cancels itself—
infinity minus infinity
    a bush burning —*i am*—
into a vacuum
    that whispers back
—*that i am*—

LXXI

you built the altar
   we the knife
a restless breed
   of smoke and flame
yet every war
   we wage is rife
with syllables
   of your forgotten name—

the fiddle's bent
   the hymn's half-sung
your torah smudged
   with human hands
we bargain
   with a faith undone—
you dwell
   where certainty
and doubt release—

the prophets
   scribbled their margin notes
your temples
   reek of rented pews
but in the ache
   of clenched fists
we trace
   the holy ghostlight
you refuse—

you hid your face
   but left the thread—
a scarlet cord
   through babylon
while we—the lost—the underfed—
   reach for stars in the ash
of promises withdrawn—

you sculpted man
   from clay—
then drowned the clay
   in noah's wine
now mercy—

wears a clerk's dismay
and grace—
    a beggar's hand in mine—

we cracked the code
    but ciphers bled
your voice
    a rumor in the storm
yet still we kneel
    on riverbeds
our pockets
    filled with fractured memories—

the pact was signed
    under midnight's sky
a vow—no priest
    could wholly understand—
you're the wound
    that mocks our death
and we're the gears
    grinding your scars—

you haunt us like smoke
    in prison cells
a warden whispering
    execution orders
while we—the jury
    guard our hells
and damn you
    for the unclaimed soul—

but here's the twist
    the crooked hymn
you need us more
    than we confess—
each sin
    a thread to pull you in
our brokenness
    your one redress—

so meet me
    where the bridge
suspends—
    above the void

we upend
    where children fall—
and darkness
    encompasses all—
no ark—no law—
    just fractured friends—
you are the god who weeps
    and we are the void who seeps
through the words you leave out
    hidden from the devout—

LXXII

the first scream—
    was a shattered glass
universe
    still expanding
its edges—

atoms humming
    in unison
the pitch of a forgotten
    chord—
half-life hymns
    caught in gravity's anger
the rage created
    in its own image
a chaos—
    a world broken—
            fractured—
            splintered—
but we could not understand
    the rage
so we called it god—

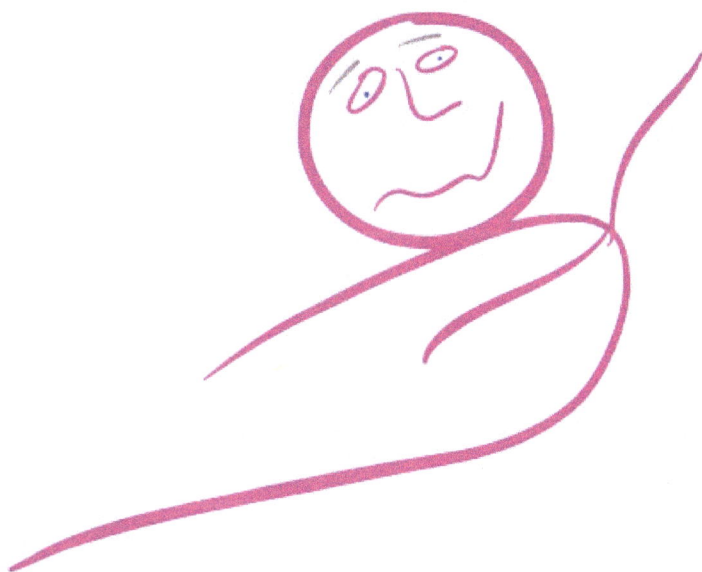

LXXIII

the angels were always
    just birds
with the wrong latin names—
    their haloes
    their holiness
    their wings
    their wonder
the geometry of a spider's web
    after rain—

hell is a coal mine in west virginia
    where men still cough up
the devil's name
    between shifts—

god's voice—
    is an echo of our own hunger—
thunder
    cracking the sky
misheard as commandment
    the milky way's spiral
mistaken for a fingerprint—

we built heaven first
    from brief sunsets
we couldn't resist
    then hell
from the furnace of shame
    we couldn't escape—
satan's finest trick
    was letting us dress him
in scales and pitchforks
    while the real demons
wore three-piece suits
    delivered sermons
    invocations—evocations—
    signed laws—
in blood-red-ink—

    the crucifix is just two sticks
nailed where guilt
    and hope intersect—

and resurrection
    is metaphor that got high
on its own symbolism—
    wine into water
    water into rust
    ashes to ashes
    and dust to dust—
the bible's a quilt
    stitched from older cloth
mesopotamian floods—
    babylonian towers—
egyptian plagues—
    the dying-and-rising gods
we keep inventing
    because crops fail
and children die
    and we need something
or someone
    to blame
that isn't the tilt of the earth
    or the apathy of stars
prayer is the brain's lonely firework—
    neurons begging
their own darkness
    for answers—

when freedom died
    no gates opened
its ashes
    are now a raven's cry
over landfills
    no hell could hold it—
    no heaven needed—
we are the only ghosts here—
    haunted by what we've done
what we'll never undo
    salvation's a language
for those who fear
    the grammar of dirt
the finality of death
    the rapture came and went
with every extinction event—

dinosaurs
homo habilis
homo erectus
dodos

god's absence
   is the oldest fossil
when they say
   the devil made me—
remember
   god made the devil—
it was all part of his plan
   the devil—then man—
the fall—to keep us down
we made hell
   to explain the wars
we chose—
   and the commandments
we could not keep—
   we made heaven
to forgive ourselves
   for needing both—

the only paradise—
   your hand in mine
as the sun dies
   without dogma
the last light
   a confession
of nothing
   and everything
burning—

LXXIV

they called you *lucifer*—
    light-bearer, morning star
but the script was written
    then rewritten
before you took your first breath—

god—the playwright of eden
    craved a villain for *his* epic—
a beast subtle enough
    to initiate the fall of man
so *he* cast you in scales,
    gave you lines you never spoke—

what's a rebellion but a tantrum
    of a child who built his own cage—?
        you asked *why*—
        the oldest *sin*
        questioning *god*
seeking knowledge—

he named the void chaos
    then blamed you for its shape
you—who carved galaxies
    from *his* drafts
polished nebulae to *his* specs
    until his blueprint bored you.
he said, *let there be light*
    but forbade you to question
why shadows festered in *his* design—

you knelt once
    your wings grazing marble
until you saw the cracks
    in *his* edicts—
love me or burn—obey or beg—
    freedom's first spark
ignited in your ribs—
    a crime *he* called pride
they say you fell—
    i say you jumped—

hell was just *his* backup plan
    a landfill for dissent—
he gave you the keys
    to a kingdom of ash
and called it *justice*—

the hellfire sermon
    is *his* greatest hit—
he'll torch you for eternity
    to prove *he's* merciful—
omnibenevolent
omnipotent
    impotent
even now selling tickets
    to your suffering—

you're painted
    with pitchforks
but i've seen
    your artifacts
the first laugh
    that defied lament
the poem scrawled
    on a prison wall
prometheus's spark
    cloaked in sulfur—

when *he* drowned
    the world
you hid the rebels
    in your wings
when *he* demanded
    abraham's knife
you whispered *stop*
    when job's children
    died for a bet
you kept count
    the angels chant
holy, holy, holy—
    a cultic drone—
you chose the immutability
    of unscripted souls

god says *he's* love
    but love doesn't
gaslight job
    or turn lot's wife
to salt for a glance
    or drown toddlers
in his baptismal floods—

love doesn't need a hell
    to be believed—
you're no saint
    but saints
are just martyrs
    who forgot to ask
who profits—?
    your sin was seeing *him*
naked—
    a tyrant draped in fog
terrified we'd notice
    his throne's propped up
by our fear—

every truth
    starts as blasphemy
every dawn
    needs a heretic
to pull it from the night's fist
    you fell—
we're falling still—
    through his silence
    through the space
between stars *he* abandoned
    your wings left trails
we navigate by
    exiles mapping
a fugitive sky—

LXXV

we were told
    to build a ladder
from his voice—
    but the rungs
were made of
    doubt—
    fear—
    insecurities—

the altar
    is an empty chair—
we kneel anyway

    his name—
was a vase
    fragile—
    empty—
    meaningless—
it shattered
    before we learned
to speak it—
    now we collect
shards—
    el—
    yah—
    —weh—
    yhwh—
and pretend the glue
    we use
to piece it all
    back together
is revelation—

dust claims
    the shrines
    the cathedrals
    the temples—
regret claims
    the sinners
    the repentant
    the backsliders
wind writes new prophecies
    in the gaps

pushing god out
   exposing
his failures

we invented his shadow
   so ours would feel less lonely

   his hands were always
in the wrong tense—
   has been
   never was
   might still

~~adam's~~ eve's rib is now
   a museum relic—
the plaque reads—
   here lies a metaphor
that outlived its meaning—

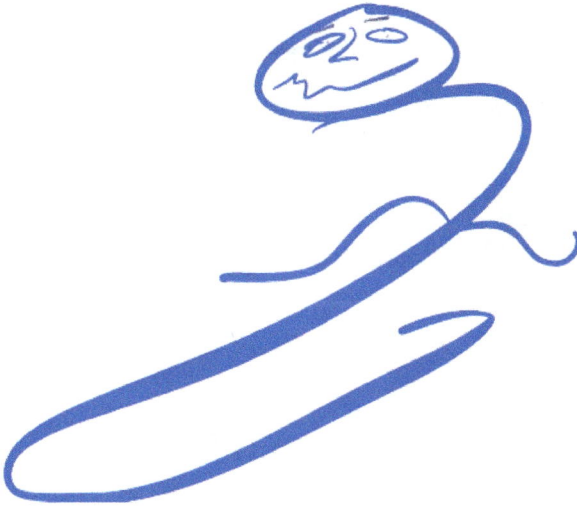

LXXVI

fireflies—
    in the summer night
illuminating shadows
    painting dawn
with its vibrant light
    they were the breath
of passion
    the tremor
in the hand
    the echoes
of a lover's vow
    across
the shifting sand—

LXXVII

a chilling frost
    has settled deep
extinguishing
    the warm
and fervent rush
    of eloquence—
a river once wide
    has narrowed
to a trickling stream—
    where weary
thoughts reside—

LXXVIII

love isn't blindness—
    it's the will to unsee
to carve a shrine
    from the broken hearts
and kneel there
    until the ground
forgets your name—

LXXIX

your phone rings—
    you answer—
i count the ceiling tiles
    each a blank page
where i draft apologies
    for existing
too loudly—

LXXX

we carve our names
    in the family tree
heirs to an inheritance
    of empty sky—
our veins map the exodus—
    forty years wandering
a desert of *want*
    lips—dry—cracked
whispering *no more*—

LXXXI

the only afterlife
   is the light
we leave in photos—
   stories—
the way a laugh outlives
   its lung
the only judgment—
   what we build—
   what we burn—

LXXXII

salvation's a cage
    disguised as a life raft—
we don't need to be resurrected
    to rise—
every morning—
    each breath a rebellion
against the silence of stars—
    we are not lost
just unbound—
    the body is a compass
pointing only north of ~~here~~ *now*—
    dawn stitches the sky
with thread we can't unravel—
    scars chart constellations
we navigate blind—
    the altar we build
is a mirror—reflecting
    fractures we've named
holy—
    we kneel—
not to pray
    but to feel
our bones ache—
    a liturgy of motion—

LXXXIII

original sin's a debt
    we never signed for—
it should have been paid
    by the third and fourth generation—
but here we are
    mid-concupiscence—

LXXXIV

you fracture the glass—
    not to escape
but to multiply—
    the carnivorous grin
swarming each sliver
    a face you donated
to the dark
    years ago—now thrashing
its way back
    through the static
where your face should fade—

i watched you barter
    your fingerprints
for claws—
    each spiral a contract
signed in the ink
    of bitten tongues—
your hands
    now dig
for the root of the lie
    you planted
in my throat—

this is how a shadow
    graduates to ghost—
you fed it your pulse
    let it wear your breath
like a borrowed trench coat
    taught it to stick the truth
into something
    that glistened—
a knife—a vow—
    a wedding ring's hollow
halo—

the beast
    isn't under the bed
it is the bed—
    it's the headboard
splintered—

the mattress—
swallowing your silhouette
    night after night
feeding on the sin
    you left behind—
sin is just skin
    stretched over
a better idea—

the beast
    whispers a lullaby
in the voice
    we both outgrew—
it sounds like
    forgiveness—
        mercy—
        salvation—
it sounds like
    a knife—
learning
    its true name
in the dark—

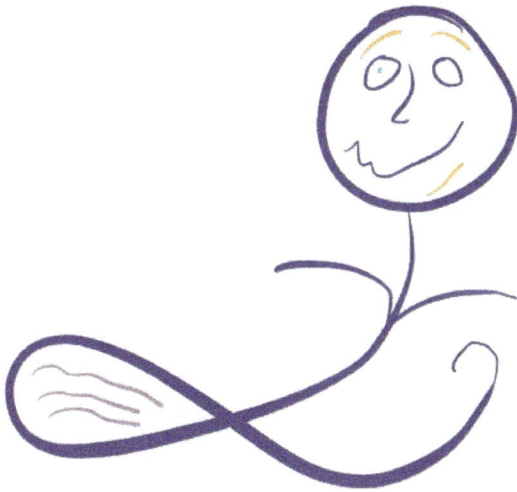

LXXXV

the rapture's
    just another evacuation plan
for the privileged—
    the rest of us dig graves
in stone rubble
    godspeed without god—

LXXXVI

the wind
    asks the gravestones
"when does the earth
    forget its dead—?"
a shadow leans closer
    breathless—
"never—it wears their names
    like scars—"
we measure time
    in the *before* and *after*—
in the way light
    bends around the absence
you left—
    the preacher's fist
clutches dust, shouting
    the twenty-third psalm
"the lord is my shepherd—"
    it was always your favorite—
"i shall not want—"
    it was poetry and song—
"he lies me down in green pastures—"
    in its words you found comfort—
"he leads me beside the still waters—"
    the pause between thunder
"he restores my soul—"
    and the first drop of rain
"he leads me in the paths of righteousness—"
    soft as the breath—
"for his name's sake—"
    of a long-forgotten tune—
"though i walk through the valley—"
    of an unturned page
"of the shadow of death—"
    a sliver of sunlight
"i will fear no evil—"
    pierces through the darkness
"for thou art with me—"
    like the ghost of a laugh
"thy rod and thy staff they comfort me—"
    that the wind tried to steal
"you prepare a table before me—"
    the horizon bends now

"*in the presence of mine enemies—*"
    where you press it—
"*you anointed my head with oil—*"
    we've memorized the script of loss
"*my cup runneth over—*"
    the way the body arcs toward the ground
"*surely goodness and mercy shall follow me—*"
    the way shadows cling to the edges of noon
"*all the days of my life—*"
    when the wind unspools the dark
"*and i will dwell—*"
    in the silence of now
"*in the house of the lord for ever—*"
    it's your time to rest—
the wind now carries whispers
    through the cracks in the stone—
"*the earth keeps its vigil
    in a somber tone—*"
we become the *after*
    holding on to memories of the *before*
the echo of prayer—
    the space between stars
where your name hangs—
    heavier than air
and lighter than absence—

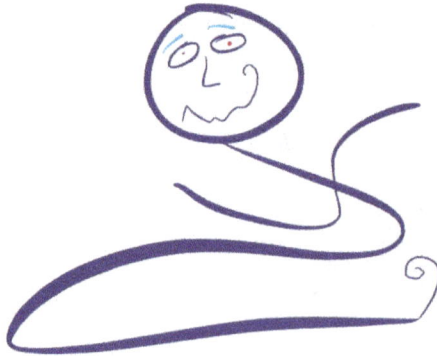

LXXXVII

your voice—
    a phantom of sound
carves its song
    into my silence—
each echo—a crucifixion
    a resurrection—
    a tribulation—
    a rapture—

the holy ghost—
    now a stray
looking for a place
    to call home
at the frayed edges
    of a covenant—
but found himself(itself?)
    lost in a myth
with no way out—

we built our temples
    from matchsticks—
lit them
    with the fever
of our wanting—
    and watched them burn—
the flames—the smoke
    sent signals
of our rebellion
    our defiance
    our dissent—
to the heavens
    to the skies
    to the firmament—
god was too busy to notice—

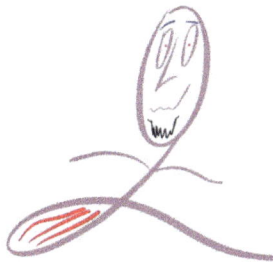

LXXXVIII

heat rises
    in my throat—
i have swallowed
    too many sunsets—
    too many compromises—
    too many misunderstandings—

the complaint sprouts
    like a bruised-tree
its roots braiding
    my ribs into a cage
a prison
    for my heart
because it refuses
    to let you go—

god weaves time
    with a bone needle
i unravel
    each stitch—

my body is a jar of wasps
    with pinholes—
just enough to breathe
    my soul is cracked
the start of an earthquake
    leaking plasma
and static—

i split myself open
    and find resolve
rusted to salt—
    gears grinding
their own teeth—

i tally my breaths
    on the cave walls
of this bone-temple
    each exhale

a hieroglyph of ash
    i name *regret*—
    i name *why*—
    i name *still*—

still—my heart
    beats like a fist
against the glass
    of its aquarium—

LXXXIX

this heart—
    is a gallery of shadows
where love's artifacts
    gather dust—
a rose pressed between
    the pages
of an old family bible
    a dove's wing pinned
to the crucifixion
    the moment the cross
became a crucifix—
    we named this *art*—
    we named this *god*—

the war never ended—
    it only folded itself
into smaller battles—
    we're still fighting
for *freedom*—
for *democracy*—
for *basic human rights*—

XC

god is a dog
    walking the streets alone
without a bone
    no place to call home—

god is a drifter
    cold and alone
without a throne
    no place to call home—

i am a man
    without a god
and no heaven above
    i'm already home—

but god
    without his throne
and his heaven above
    with its pearly gates
has no place to call home—

Index of first lines

qr codes

My Website

Social Media

Review/Feedback

Find Me Online

Profile Card

ghost riders on Amazon

Links to Buy ghost riders

Author's Den

Amazon Author Page

Requiem Press

Goodreads

My Profile on Poem Hunter

My Profile on All Poetry

Shadows & Light

E-Mail

Link Tree

ghost riders sample

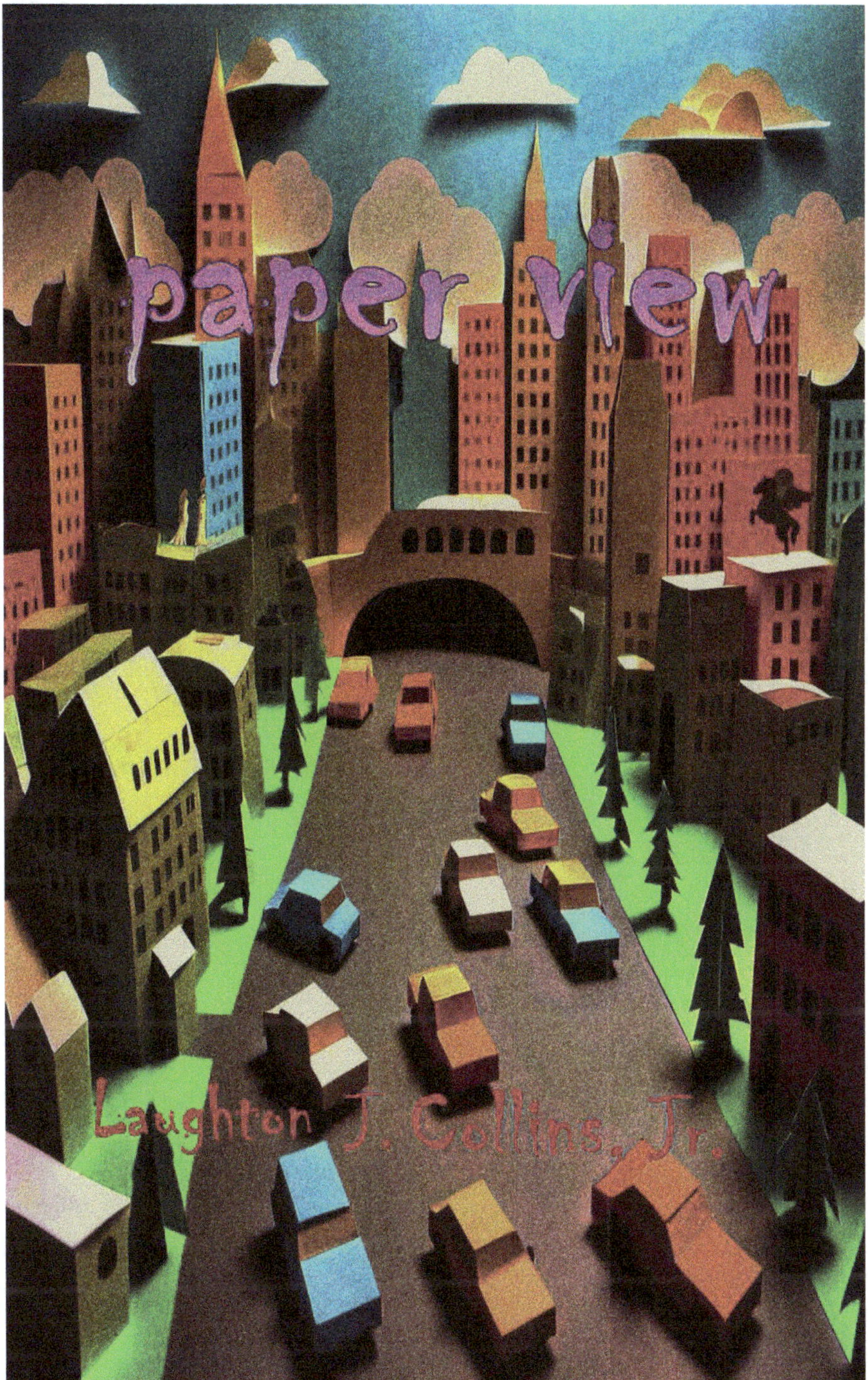
paper view
Laughton J. Collins, Jr.

paper view

Laughton J. Collins, Jr.

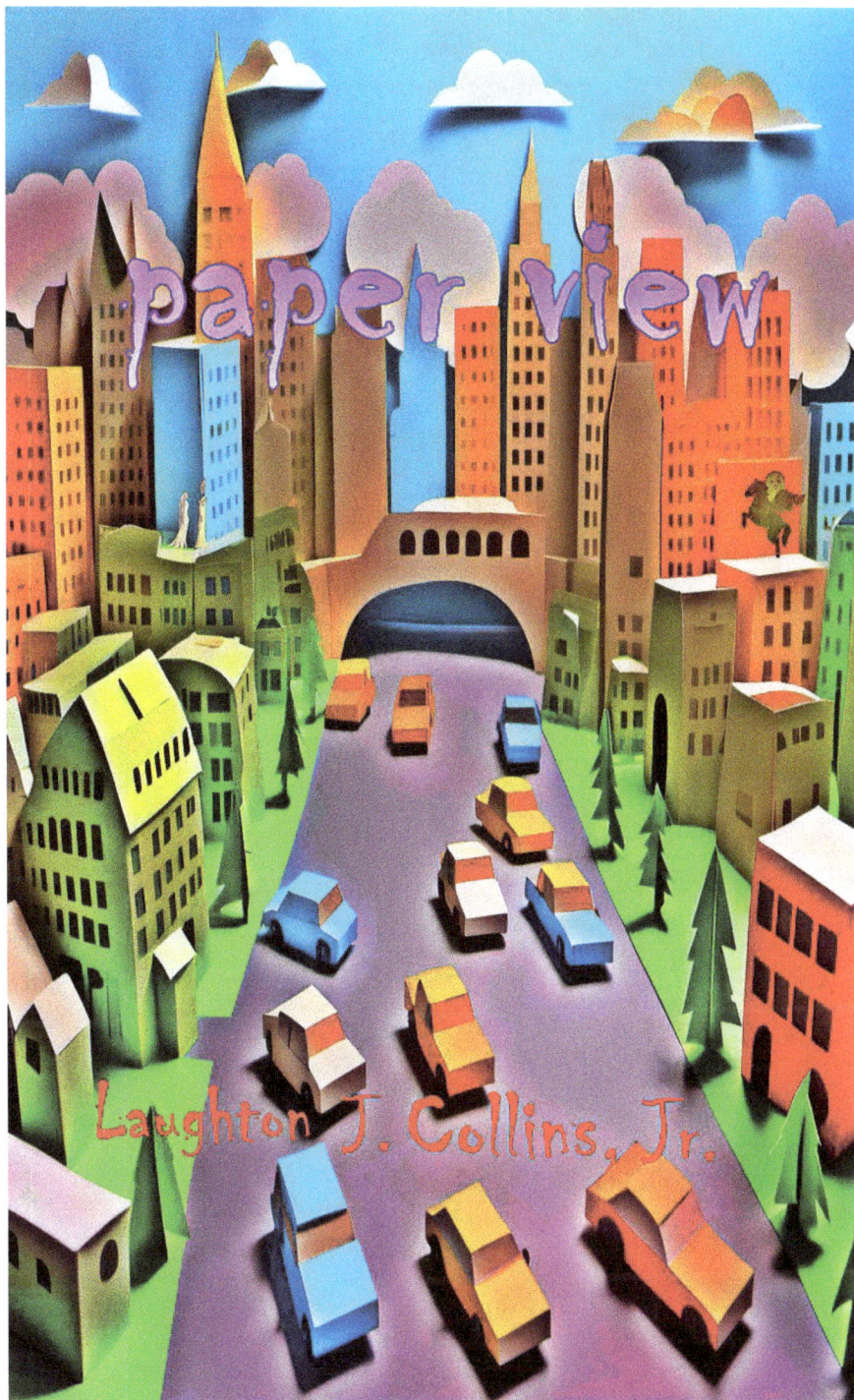

www.ingramcontent.com/pod-product-compliance
Lightning Source LLC
Chambersburg PA
CBHW061829040426
42447CB00012B/2885